Out of Body

by:
KJ GoForth

Co-author:
Adira

Gotham Books

30 N Gould St.
Ste. 20820, Sheridan, WY 82801
https://gothambooksinc.com/

Phone: 1 (307) 464-7800

© 2023 KJ GoForth. All rights reserved.

No part of this book may be reproduced, stored in a retrieval system, or transmitted by any means without the written permission of the author.

Published by Gotham Books (October 3, 2023)

ISBN: 979-8-88775-557-1 (H)
ISBN: 979-8-88775-555-7 (P)
ISBN: 979-8-88775-556-4 (E)

Because of the dynamic nature of the Internet, any web addresses or links contained in this book may have changed since publication and may no longer be valid.

The views expressed in this work are solely those of the author and do not necessarily reflect the views of the publisher, and the publisher hereby disclaims any responsibility for them.

About the Book

This is another attempt to assist in creating a perception that lies outside limits or boundaries. Our intuition and what we were born to this place to accomplish being a topic that runs throughout these rhymes.

At our core lives a wounded child whose innocence has been corrupted by a society that seeks to manipulate us into submission. The many layers of control waged against us are the very walls crafted to keep us in the dark. Colonialism's divide and conquer technique are unfortunately still with us today.

Introduction

Only through the ancient wisdom that lives in our DNA, clear visions that benefit humanity, the ability to resolve conflict through peace, an open heart that embraces our differences, and ears that have learned how to listen can humanity move past its greedy, power hungry, controlling ways. The change we search for only can come from within one person at a time. A slow and tedious process, but well worth the ride. When the word "AWE" is understood it becomes a matter of how to explain how one's life has transformed. The fearless, independent, peaceful and spiritually enlightened souls have everything needed to bring about the end of authorities lies and dogma.

Thanks again. Enjoy!

KJ

Dedicated to anyone brave enough to face their fears.

Past be the past what can we learn
When corruption leads war will burn

Static chaos justifying cause
Dogmatic religions writing our laws

Peddling influence tearing apart
The very fabric that lives in our heart

Whittling away at each soul
As leadership is digging our hole.

Freedoms not free but a right
Government clowns infringe as they bite

Left or right with their back door bomb
Laughing to myself as I stay calm

Youth in transition being true
Honor the path you came to do

Find the strength drop the mask
Free your mind have a blast

Open up life's mysteries
Bring the rain to the trees

Shelter love in your heart
Let your memories be a part

Confidence causing wholesome growth
You and me we are both

Stand up proud leaders lead
Inspire others with your seed

Fearlessly finding loads of fun
Be yourself be as one

Lingering letters tip of tongue
Shock the world you have come

Be your power let it shine
Don't be the wino drunk on wine

Weeded garden ripened fruit
Brand new season astral truth

Intuition out on point
Polished diamond every joint

Rockstar glory shocking glow
Show the world how you flow

Breath in fire exhale love
Set intention from above

Friend to many head held high
Humble enough to show a cry

Glad we met you got skill
Don't forget to just chill

Never back down, always stand tall
From every obstacle, rise up from the fall
And let your courage be your alter
In the face of fear, do not falter

In the stormy sea of life, do not lose sight
For there is a beacon that shines so bright
Of the dreams that you hold so dear
Guiding you nearer, making sight clear

So take a deep breath, raise your head high
For the greatest victory, is the one you defy
When you rise up with all your might
And face each challenge with your bright light

And when you stumble, and fall to the ground
For every time you rise, you'll become profound
Get up, brush yourself, and stand tall
And your courage will conquer them all

So never back down, in the face of strife
And in the end, your spirit will soar to new heights
For you are a warrior, bold and brave
As you rise, triumphant, from the grave

Slow down a second see what I see
Lift up your head take a peek through the trees

Come out of your cave paint a new wall
All castles crumble each one will fall

Model of plastic brittle and old
The future is ours we are the new mold

Each passing moment always in tune
No time for behavior acts the baboon

Foot on the throttle break lines been cut
Tires are all muddy out of the rut

Breakfast in bed sun on our face
Sensing it time to win the big race

Action required kick back and watch
Tongue twisted fools slurping up slop

Ready for next phase no bags required
Grow a new shell and be inspired

Smoke and mirrors distractions galore
Hide the evidence kill the core

Power struggle back and forth
No one winning same old course

Booby traps everywhere
Slaves of justice never dare

Altered image labeled box
Black and red purple sox

Tattooed symbol fettered faith
Dense destructions overweight

Rotten apples sour grapes
Blind from blinders over rates

Shifty coercion obligates
Conformity obliterates

Infused for freedom tolerate
Ignorance it's not too late

Celestial soul with free choice
Credits earned sponge is moist

Antenna tuned frequency
Love the channel for you and me

Pressure cooker mads design
Dull the finish dull the shine

Ignorance leading cause
Money grubbing avoid the laws

Holy hell sacrament
Torture terror prevalent

Eons waiting flip the switch
Ride the wave don't be a bitch

Toddlers teething bitten brood
Spread the fear kill the mood

No one's coming saving grace
The church is lying to our face

*Alone, I stand and face the day
With just my thoughts to light the way
The wind may blow, the sky may pour
But in this space, I find my roar*

*Being alone is not a curse
It gives me time to think, to verse
To find the parts of me that hide
And in this quiet, I can bide*

*I am the master of my fate
And in this solitude, I create
The world within my mind to see
A place of peace and majesty*

*The stillness gives me strength to grow
To know the things I need to know
And in this space, I find my peace
The calm that comes from being at ease*

*So let the world around me spin
I'll find my solace from within
For being alone is not a bad thing
It's a chance to spread my wings and sing*

Rise above the chaos leave the past behind
Open up your heart feel your body shine

Don't give into temptation confusion of the greed
Be grateful of your own life responsible indeed

Tear off layers confining lies
Shock yourself honest eyes

No plan to great inspiring
Why wait until nature's spring

Heart strings tugging to and fro
Know which ones need to go

Honor growth stand up tall
Make it fun have a ball

Become your new self be set free
No longer tied to conformity

Question all you've ever known
And you'll find out we're not alone

Safe bubble babies must be in the milk
Panties up the crack polyester silk

Always crying foul which feeling did it hurt
Predisposed to slavery victim in a shirt

Cradle to the grave victim and slave

Blind faith robbing scum will surely make you dumb

Feathers of a foul altered by the bowel
Translation comprised justifying lies

Riddle rhyming rules tongue
twisting all the fools

Harboring the hate brainwashing call it fate

Designate one name consolidate the grain

Path for lonely fools building full of tools

Time to run and hide religion don't provide

Bananas yellow apples red bleeding profusely
from the head

Traps and triggers all around trip wire
springing from the ground

Clogged up drains rotten fruit machoism
quit the bruit

Feminism falling flat triggered fat chicks
spewing splat

Bitch and moan pissing match just
the surface only scratch

Divided concurred barons rule enslave
the people big cesspool

Carrot dangled bound by rules generations
of more fools

Baby diaper smelly mess constitution under duress

Power proving not for me born to
freedom not conformity

Landmines laid blasting caps trigger armed
in case perhaps

Reaching for a dream, a goal in sight
With determination and will so bright
A journey ahead, filled with twists and turns
But a fire within, forever burns

A dream so big, seems sand on a beach
But with every step, it comes within reach
For every obstacle, a lesson to learn
And a new strength, for which our hearts yearn

So reach for the stars, with all your might
And never give up, without a fight
For every stumble, and every fall
Brings you closer, to the standing tall

And when you finally, reach that goal
With memories, of the battles you've known
You'll look back, with a smile so true
And know that you made, your dream come true

So keep reaching, for what you desire
And never give up, to the burning fire
For with hard work, and a steadfast heart
Your dream will come true, and a new chapter start

Heart of gold reach the shore
Treacherous journey with just one ore

Passion filled tank on full
Roll the dice ride the bull

Saddle up and hold on
Built for speed built for fun

Bod on fire lips a glow
Safely seated to watch the show

Braided beauty peaceful soul
Loving eyes with all the flow

Glancing courage out to win
Taking shots on the chin

Be yourself feel the stir
Vision clears without blur

One of a kind special blend
Keep your head up till the end

Picked on by posers burnt desire
Turned to alcohol fueling the fire

Crimped connection bordering truth
Blackout madness moral proof

Inner hostage like a scared child
Looking for freedom back to the wild

Emotional drainage broken heart
Lift up your head make a new start

Answers all buried deep within
Nothing outside will heal any sin

Each to his own time to get bold
Why do what you are told

Freedoms not free but worth the ride
Conformity kills altered in stride

Aware to do better aware to be great
Don't let opinions hold you from fate

In the darkest of times here we wait
Exercising goodness to seal evils fate

Hasn't been easy not always clear
Bumps in the path causing a veer

Switching lanes shifting gears
Seeming worth it so it appears

Negative energy feeding contempt
Dragons' breath evils intent

Respirators rescue arteries clogged
Dogmatic madness bleeding hog

Disturbing revelation poisoned well
Spreading division preaching hell

Manifesting martyrs no act too low
Justifying as it goes

History repeated ignorance rules
Digging graves for the fools

*The place we met the sun we share
The puzzle pieces the perfect pair*

*Lifetimes of Conection's forever friends
A dependable love that never ends*

*Starry eyes with a dreamy vibe
A loving heart with wisdom to guide*

*As castaways in an unknown land
In bare feet with toes in the sand*

*Entangled in a dance we know so well
Consumed by love and its spell*

*The price of admission worth the wait
When the love we give brings good fate*

Great things take time, they say
It grows slowly day by day
As the seed becomes a tree
Patiently, it's meant to be

The masterpiece you seek to make
It's born with every move you take
Is not an overnight task
And every question that you ask

The artist's brushstroke, precise
As the colors mix, and they rise
Each stroke deliberate and slow
Their beauty starts to show

The writer's pen on paper flows
As every word and line it knows
A story woven, thread by thread
Will lead the reader ahead

The builder's hands, they work with care
The structure grows, with patience rare
Brick by brick, and stone by stone,
Till it becomes a place called home

Great things take time, it's true
The effort that you put into
As every moment counts
Will bring the best amounts

So, take the time to create
For every step that you take
And never give up the fight
Let your passion lead you to the light

Status symbol status quo
External world without much soul

Copy the jones material wealth
Tied to possessions bloated health

Slave so hard get ahead
Maggot feeding on its bread

Subvert the law or pay the man
Criminals control across the land

Equal rights under the law
If only you'd seen what I saw

The wheels turning tipping point
washing clean every joint

So do the work feel the glow
I can say I told you so

Pope-ity dope-ity had a great fall
Pope-ity dope-ity fell off its wall

Now all the pope's friars and all its bishops
Could not restore order to all that it worships

The blasphemous lies the negative cries

The justified line the poisonous wine

The black mail and fear its
mercenaries revere

The guilt casting clown the stain on your town

The beheadings galore the criminal deplore

The dark shady acts with blood on its ax

The greedy taxation oldest mafia sensation

Why say more stop enabling the whore

Paradigm full of slime

Dead weight dogs fat like hogs

Smelly swine drunk on wine

Authority controlling thee

Jump point black smoking crack

False in fiction damned conviction

Brain wash brine dying vine

Buried stool drink ass fool

Salvation sickness moral witness

Breaking stride no need to hide

Hollow heart envious tart

Denials face killing our race

To survive is to rise, in the face of the storm
To hold on to hope, when everything seems forlorn
To find the strength within, to endure and overcome
And to keep moving forward, until the battle is won

The journey may be tough, with obstacles to face
But with a resilient spirit, we can conquer any race
For every challenge we overcome, we grow stronger
And with each hurdle we clear, we endure longer

Surviving is not just about living through the pain
But about learning to thrive, even in the pouring rain
It's about finding the light, when darkness descends
And holding on to faith, until the bitter end

For every scar we bare, is a testament to our strength
A reminder of the battles we've fought, no matter the length
And in the end, it's the warriors who survive
Who emerge victorious, and truly come alive
So let us embrace the struggle, and face it with courage
For surviving is not just about getting through the wreckage

But about emerging from the fire, with a heart that's brave
And a spirit that's unbreakable, even in the darkest of days

Ism you is or ism you ain't
Ism for life ready to faint

So many ism's so little time
Choosing my favorite which one to rhyme

Behavioral study labeling code
Statistical model pot holey road

Brandishing bullets full metal jacket
Eating away societies fabric

Are joyous journey finding some truth
Wisdom behold plenty of proof

Each era tainted each era blind
Conformity stealing most of our shine

Repressed reprogrammed pause mode revealed
Take a look around what do you feel

Under the thumb under the boot
Birds in the air here's my salute

Righteous moral high ground safe behind the cross
Heavy justification scruples of the lost

Backward from the start smelling like a fart

Party favorites altar boys
Place trust where sickening noise

Another excuse another wrong
Ignorance just keep moving along

The serpent's head has grown strong
It eats its young but not for long

The gig is up the game is over
No more fear no four leaf clover

I'll be laughing with the ants
Watching power piss it's pants

Synced to sound vibrate
Humble and honest liberate

Forthright flowing tide pool calm
Mystic beginning read the palm

Algerythisms scientific turds
De bacherie of our words

Relic nation admires itself
Ill intentions balloted health

Pacifier in its mouth
Gobbling gobble up our wealth

Good intentions gone awry
Rich get richer while poor die

Callus empire stolen land
Cut the hand off from the man

Self-entitled codependency
Worry some never free

Light a candle feel the glow
Be the star of your own show

Rest easy dear soul I've got your back
Congratulations for fighting off the attack

Trapped in that heart that you hold
Are cures for medicine I am told

A treasure chest of wisdom and wealth
I am manifesting your wellness and health

Your strength is bold your presence grand
Your gifts are deep from where I stand

Your fires been lit from the spark of life
There will be no more of the strife

Here for you a shoulder for tears
And a heart of gold that knows no fears

In the face of the odds, our spirit shines bright
A beacon of hope, in the darkest of nights
For we refuse to be beaten, by the trials we face
And choose to rise above them, with courage and grace

Our spirit is a flame, that burns bright and strong
Even when the road ahead seems uncertain and long
It's a force that pushes us forward, towards the light
And helps us find the way, even in the darkest of nights.

For we know that within us, lies a strength and power
A force that can conquer any challenge or tower
And we choose to harness it, with every breath we take
And use it to conquer, any obstacle in our wake.

With a high spirit, we face the world head on
No fear or doubt, can hold us down for long
For we know that with every step we take
We're one step closer, to the dreams we want to make

So let us hold on to that high spirit, and never let it go
For it's the key to overcoming, any obstacle or foe
And with it, we can achieve, anything we set our mind to
And rise above the odds, to make our dreams come true

*I pray this prayer through these tears
I give this life without fears*

*Been held back far too long
Now I'm growing ever strong*

*Committed to truth humbling awe
Thankful for all that I have saw*

*Honored the process test of tests
Producing goodness at my best*

*Barriers gone flowing free
Being who I'm supposed to be*

*Gratefully guided protected too
Choosing only you know who*

*Tattered t-shirts working hands
Not afraid to take a stand*

*Silent suffering go away
Your days are over it's time to play*

Living in the moment being who I am
Big plans for the future diving off a dam

In the greatness because I can
Avoiding scumbags and life's big scam

Tuner tuned in frequency
Laughing playing fun for me

Trouble distant memories
Soaring silent through the trees

Character growing how I choose
Defining choices no more blues

No more backward bitter mess
Time to roost and create a nest

Holy moly peter pan
Found a purpose yes I can

Friend or foe menace to man
From the start how chaos began

Indoctrination to slavery
Religion and its pious greed

Wealthy warlands conquering
Fertial neighbors surrounding

Nothings changed nothing new
Supremacy for the few

At god's speed take them to someplace
Heal the people heal our race

Be our beacon be our hope
Tie the hands up of the pope

Give us back what we deserve
Reinstruct us how to serve

Sail our ships into safe harbors
Groom us like our local barbers

Colors dance upon the canvas bright
Infinite hues of the rainbow's light
A symphony of shades in endless flight
Painting a portrait of pure delight

Golden rays of sunshine warm the earth,
A mellow yellow, full of mirth,
Orange blazing with passion's fire
Like the warmth of a lover's desire

Red as a rose, passion and love
Like a heart on fire, soaring above
Purple, regal in all its glory
Majestic and bold, its story

Blue, calm as the ocean deep
A serene tranquility weaved and steeped
Green, a lush and fertile land
Life and growth, on which we stand

Colors meld and blend and fuse
A kaleidoscope of beauty that doth amuse
From vibrant hues to subtle pastels
Each color holds its own sweet spells

Consult the conscience to explore
Our true nature we've all bore

Get in touch feel the flow
Stretch the body begin to grow

Cast off shadows negativity
Breath in deep plant new seed

Shock the core lift your head
Bleed the words out that's been bleed

Martyr kingdom coincides
While wicked black wolves claw our sides

Darkness dancing in white robes
Leading humanity down dead end roads

Free your mind free your soul
Feed the white wolf let him glow

Earn your wings they're yours to have
Don't let conformity steal your good half

Mis managed energy dirty with dust
Lonesome and sad sick from lust

Standing for one martyr for all
Behind the eight ball ready to fall

Poised and primed spiritual suicide
Religious divisions do provide

Noxious odor in the air
Providing sickness do I dare

Belly to the bar drunk in line
Sunday service slurping wine

Someone help me I'm insane
Cleanse my body in acid rain

Laugh out loud just my way
Exist in the moment everyday

My beautiful Angel matapang
Hear my heart hear its song

I sing it loud out in the rain
It is not sad it has no pain

A hearts desire deserving strength
Be the one that I can thank

Parachute open no free fall
Gliding safely to it all

Imagination free to roam
Let us build a brand new home

This is our place and our time
We the one I write this rhythm

A golden heart I give to you
Be my queen I love you.

Beyond the bounds of what was thought
A spark of greatness in you caught
You soared above and rose to new heights
Breaking free from old limits and rights

You've surpassed what was expected
And journeyed beyond the projected
With strength and skill you've climbed the peak
Proving there is nothing you cannot seek

The world is wide, the journey long
But in your heart, you hear your song
That drives you forward, ever strong
The desire to achieve what once seemed wrong

Your courage and resilience inspire
As you climb higher and never tire
To show that greatness lies within
And with hard work, we all can win

You have exceeded every expectation
With perseverance and dedication
And shown the world what we can be
A shining example for all to see

Monotheistic alluring bait
Tyrants bullying forcing fate

Trinity and tyranny
Never enough never free

Sucking sensation eagerly
Robs the goodness from you and me

Narrative null and void
Keep your distance will avoid

Broken windows hollow shell
No wonder criminals created hell

Beat back opposition can't resist
No low to low for the fist

The black plague has no need
It can't compete with right hand seed

Talking points bla bla bla
There all wrong ha ha ha

Hold me tight I'm all alone
Stand beside me on our thrown

Be my hearts closest desire
Stoke the flames of this fire

Bring your beauty bring your strength
These words to you are my thanks

No matter nothing no matter none
Be my queen let's get 'er done

As I profess as I concede
You're the one the one I need

One of a kind a sacred shell
I'm your pearl let's ring the bell

What's mine is yours your is mine
Feel that tingle down your spine

Hard to handle all this love
You're my angel from above

Shoveling sh*t pond to fill
Someday religion will get its bill

Parchment paper stone tablets
Liars lying on pulpits

Dignity died on the cross
Look at all the lives its cost

Sensational story used at will
Justifying all its ill

Printed paper scorched earth approach
Who's the heathen who's the roach

Backward brain washed belligerent blind
All the words that define

False ego fools lecturing lunatics
Passing on falsehoods see where it sticks

Defenders of righteous sick in the head
I'll hand you a bullet it's made of lead

Snowbird sing your song of songs
Keep space clear for rights and wrongs

Keep your head up when times are tough
Don't be afraid to call out bluff

Feel your way through the stars above
Redefine the things you love

Learn the treasure you came to share
In case the mirror reflects despair

Anchor your light to the mothers core
Pay no mind to keeping score

Flow like magic with wings spread wide
And seek the wisdom you hold inside

Success cannot be weighed or measured
By mere possessions or wealth treasured
It's not the car you drive or the house you own
Nor the fame you've gained or the seeds you've sown

True success comes from the heart within
A life well-lived, a soul without sin
It's the love you give and the joy you spread
The way you help others, and the tears you've shed

It's the battles you've fought and
the scars you bare
The resilience you've shown,
the strength you share
The kindness you've offered and the
warmth you've brought
The lessons you've learned and the growth
you've sought

Success is not found in the numbers
you've amassed
Or the titles you hold or the power you've cast
It's in the way you've touched others
and left your mark
The way you've lived your life with
purpose and heart

So let us not be fooled by worldly gains
Or allow our pursuits to cause us pain
For true success is found in the person
we've become
And the legacy we leave when
our time is done.

The human mind is full of quirks
The human heart is full of perks

So easy the mind takes control
Digging humanity a deeper hole

Persecuted for free thought
Lots of wisdom I done got

Setting course thee unknown
ET needs to phone his home

Carried through the worst of times
Trust in truth riddle rhymes

No one coming to save the day
It's on us the only way

Principals not profit pass the buck
Religion has caused a lot of muck

Creature of habit poisoned wine
Not designed for us to shine

Born to be wild with a cause
Tearing down walls breaking the laws

Sickle to the serpent sever the head
Dissecting the body covered in red

Planting new seeds forbidden fruit
Freeing the minds of the youth we pollute

Digesting the downloads my friends they can't wait
All things be knowing it's not too late

Steadfast and steady cautiously climb
Rung on a ladder earning a dime

Ballbuster coming settle the score
Eager to get through the final door

Shocking revealing holding on tight
Awake to a purpose no need to fight

Stain on the mattress stain on the floor
Wake up people to whom you adore

Vicarious living time for a pause
Get out side find a good cause

End your coma stop sleepwalking
Close your mouth no one likes gawking

Wasted energy delusional faith
Materialism is its fate

Rapture rocking soul less cores
Criminals causing puss like sores

Satisfaction whats that mean
Just a cog in the machine

Guarded garden sacred soul
Misery does take its toll

Sexy symbol man on cross
Martyrism not my boss

Fluttering wings of vibrant hue
A butterfly emerges anew
From caterpillar to graceful flight
A metamorphosis so wondrously bright

In gardens and fields it dances and sways
A symbol of hope in its delicate ways
A creature of beauty, a symbol of change
An inspiration to us in a world so strange

Its wings to carry on a gentle breeze
A sight that brings us to our knees
For in the butterfly we see
The power of transformation and beauty

So let us cherish this fleeting delight
The butterfly, a wonder in flight
For it reminds us to embrace the new
And to find beauty in all we pursue

Bribed and blackmailed pecking order
Behind a desk giving off oder

Spewing madness from your hole
Time to flush the toilet bowl

Waders on chest deep high
Shit keeps coming wonder why

Top to bottom primed to purge
Collapse be coming on the verge

Where's my hall pass gotta go
Center stall in back row

Leaky seal gasket blown
In the future I was shown

Pesky piss ants passing by
Light your liters one last goodbye

Virus message soaked in guilt
Look at the kingdoms it did built

Terrorizing colonies claiming as own
How power controls far from its home

Mercenaries first missionaries second
Robbing and pillaging every second

Hosting conformity controlling its words
This has the smell of big turds

Poking its nose into others paths
I hope someones watching to dole out the rath

Bloodshed at hand a stones throwaway
This is religion in its hay day

Authoritarian clergy bent on its power
It's still here wrecking the hour

Mana bread kept them fed
Days of moses so it's said

Professional victim hood in this day
On the train carried away

Crying foul while stealing your wood
Pious descendants never could

Chose for what I wanna know
Control the world's wealth in gold

How about diamonds or precious jewels
House of cards fools rules

Bed of nails or hot coals
Bong the gong pay the tolls

Payment overdue for pious greed
Poisoned ground dying seed

Orthodox or otherwise
Lights are out in the eyes

Standing at the edge looking down
No turning back left that town

Hoping for wings after the fall
This head is tired from banging the wall

Each and every inch refines
No human head could ever define

The plastic bucket fills with soil
As war rages over lands with oil

Industry booms as bombs are built
Authority denies the blood it's spilt

Kingdoms clergy empires rocked
Bullet in the chamber and the hammer is cocked

Disappointment and appointments
Two words that seem so distant
But in truth, they are intertwined
In the chaos of the human mind

We set our goals, we make our plans
We try to take life in our own hands
We book our meetings, make our dates
And hope that fate, for us, awaits

But often, things don't go as planned
Our dreams fall short, our hopes unmanned
The appointments we made,
so well in advance
Turn into disappointment, and we're left to chance

We feel the weight, of our own expectations
And suffer the pain, of our own frustrations
But in the midst of our darkest hour
We can still find the strength, to muster our power

For disappointment, is not the end
But a chance for us, to try again
To learn from our mistakes, and rise rebirthed
To face our fears, and not feel blue

So embrace disappointment, and let it be
An opportunity, for you to see
That appointments may fail, and plans may fall
But you still have the power, to stand tall

Preclandestine whos to blame
Dry your eyes this worlds insane

Hook in the mouth of a big whale
Conformity slavery what the hell

Up from a nightmare treading in sync
Blackout over now on the brink

Transition facade marriage of the past
Blaming no more strength to last

No cost too high no mountain too tall
Going the distance not gonna fall

Vicariously positioned sailing clear
Nothing will catch me especially fear

Send out the soldier's arm then well
Dig your trenches straight to hell

Weakened feeble victim hood
Now you know understood

Up all night pupils shot
Bad ass headache is what I got

Cocaine cowboy life for me
Running wild running free

Girls so fine barely dressed
Sexy creatures baring breasts

Another rail hold on tight
Brain gone numb on me tonight

One way ticket to the moon
Cocaine drug store coming soon

Vitamin C the cure to all ails
Peruvian highway brings in bails

Sike not current but sure was fun
That life is over new one begun

In a land of giggles, where humor reigns
With Funny poetry and laughter sustains
A lighthearted jest and comedic delight
Let's embark on a journey tonight

Once a snail named Fred, oh so slow
Competed in a race, as the crowd did grow
But alas, he crossed the finish line last
Exclaiming, "I won, the Tortoise was fast!"

In a zoo, monkey with a cheeky grin
Swung from vines, creating quite a din
He grabbed a hat placed it on his head
Becoming a fashionista, "Monkey Chic," he said

A clumsy penguin, wobbling on ice
Tripped and slipped, his movements imprecise
He slid into a snowman, much to his dismay
Apologized, "Oops, Frosty, have a nice day!"

A chicken, ambitious, dreamed of flight
Built a rocket, determined to sore out of sight
But as it took off, feathers went astray
Clucking, "Guess gravity wanted her to stay!"

Now, a joke for you, to bring a smile
Why did the tomato turn red with style?
Because it saw the salad dressing!
Oh, what a pun
A chuckle-worthy punchline, laughter to be spun.

So let humor be our guide, in this funny spree
With laughter as our compass, hearts full of glee
For in this playful world, where jokes take flight
We'll find endless amusement, oh what a delight

Gaping hole serenade
One of a kind how I was made

Inspiring change life without
Pain and suffering or any doubt

Easy easy old guard dies
Seeing through all its lies

Criminal kingdom on our shores
No respect only whores

Pride and honor gone extinct
Hostile occupation before we blink

Way of life spiritual ways
Laying dormant for quite some days

Many moons many seasons
Asking creator for the reasons

War paint with a smiling mask
Liberation all we ask

Not invited not a guest
Final moments of the big quest

Shoot the messenger I got news
Organize religion is confused

The flock it runs to and fro
Never knowing which way to go

Trail of tears all over again
Every generation all over sin

Where's the vision where's the focus
Materialism devours like locus

Fearful of a made up place
Control the masses such a disgrace

Table scraps bottom feeder
One man dies he's the bleeder

Sensationalism imagery
Scam of all scams butchery

Walk a straight line to find out
We are much more than they tout

Spiritual at our core
Not salvation what a bore

As the day draws near its gentle close
Sunset arrives as a soothing dose
A remedy for the weary soul's plight
In hues of gold and pink, a tranquil sight

With each stroke of the sun's descending glow
A remedy for the heart to truly know
A respite from the chaos of the day
As nature paints its serene display

The sky ablaze with fiery hues
Sunset's remedy brings a tranquil muse
A moment to breathe, to let worries cease
As the world slows down and finds its peace

The crimson clouds, a healing balm
Sunset's remedy, a soothing calm
A gentle reminder of life's fleeting grace
Embracing solace in this sacred space

In the warm embrace of twilight's embrace
Sunset's remedy brings serenity and grace
A time to reflect, to heal and restore
As day bids farewell and night takes its chore

So let the sunset's colors wash over you
Let its remedy mend and renew
Find solace in the fading light
As the sunset whispers
"Everything will be alright"

Brutally honest to a flaw
But it doesn't break the law

Every aspect every curve
Now I want what we deserve

It's not respect or dignity
It's what was taken from you and me

Recognition of what's gone wrong
And who's the singer of this song

Step right up enjoy the show
Watch the spectacle it won't blow

Sideways steering tailgate
Walls exploding can hardly wait

Blocking traffic warning sign
Deaf and dumber lead the blind

Attacks are staged to commence
Song birds singing on the fence

Just a moment and look up
Passions spilling from this cup

On the verge of something amazing
While the sheep are a grazing

Distracted by what seems green fields
The grass is dying as power yields

Separation from the source
There's no saddle for that horse

Ride em bronco get bucked off
Pain and anger with a cough

Unstable blocks leaning tower
End of the line the last hour

Shock waves tremors salivate
Weight been lifted rocked by fate

Envy burning in the fields
Hiding behind word like shields

Later losers last in line
Maybe next time you may shine

Demeaning words not good enough
Toxic talk down give a stuff

Condemnation belligerent
Believing lies ignorant

Condescending burrade the youth
Pitched up high on triangular roof

Conceded controlling life times past
This time we remove the mask

Who's that person labeling
Children love it on a swing

Freewill living on this page
Excitement building grand the stage

Pure and polished light shines through
Doing what was meant to do

Collapse the cartel free the soul
Too many years has had its toll

Upon the horizon, stands the last mountain tall
Its majestic silhouette, a grandeur to enthral
A solitary sentinel, against the endless sky
A symbol of resilience, towering up high

Its ancient peaks kissed by the sun's golden hue
Veiled in clouds and mist, a mystical view
Guardian of nature, keeper of secrets untold
Whispering tales of wisdom, as the years unfold

Its slopes adorned with forests,
lush and green
Where mighty rivers flow, pure and pristine
Creatures of the wild find refuge in its embrace
Finding solace and freedom,
in this sacred space

The last mountain beckons, with a silent plea
"Come, wanderer, explore and set your spirit free
Uncover the mysteries that lie within
Embrace the beauty, let your adventure begin"

With each step forward, the air grows thin
As if ascending to realms where dreams begin
The challenges mount, steep paths to climb
Yet the allure of the summit transcends all time

Through valleys and ridges,
where echoes rebound
A quest for enlightenment,
in silence profound
Every footfall echoes with stories of the past
Of intrepid explorers, whose memories will last

Do you have a qualm about your past
What about that cross tattooed on your ass

What obscure meaning did coercion cause
Doing it's best finding your flaws

Extorsion the pay off blackmail the scheme
Oh my goodness what have I seen

Destiny dancing all out of breathe
You make the call you be the reff

Strangle the will choke off the source
All because power it's plan of course

Eat from ills table supper at last
Or give it the finger and go have a blast

Disturbing confession won't hesitate
Knowing the meaning of alienate

Celebrate new freedom illusion gone
Chess board is clear no longer a pawn

A tender touch with enchanted smile
Desirable smell untapped vile

Brilliant and poised easy to trust
Respectable humble sensual lust

Determined polite loving and calm
She the full package she be da bomb

Unique and pure passionate glow
Minds been blown this I know

Serious creation not messing around
Blessed angel sweet voice sound

Tantalizing body respectable
Beautiful mind loving soul

Creative caring reasonable
Determined always to let love grow

Refreshing image in my dream
It's all been worth it so it does seem

Past is over blink of an eye
In your face staying high

High on life Instead of drugs
Independent No AA hugs

Tentacle of the right
Born again not so bright

Codependent once again
Score kept switching death within

Not born to follow not born to lead
Not born to die of senseless need

Critical thinking mystic mind
Humanity has gone blind

Material relish serve the self
Boasting bragging beloded wealth

Sorry sucker seen your show
It's a rerun time to go

In the hush of darkness, when stars shine bright
The world surrenders to the enchantment of night
A canvas of ebony, adorned with twinkling grace
Midnight begins, unveiling a mystic embrace

The clock strikes twelve, and silence takes hold
As dreams awaken, their stories unfold
Midnight, the threshold to a realm untamed
Where possibilities bloom, and desires are named

Whispers in shadows, secrets to be told
As moonbeams dance, casting secrets in bold
The night's symphony, a chorus unseen
Where hearts find solace, in twilight's serene

From the depths of darkness, new journeys arise
A symphony of hopes, where the spirit flies
The chimes of midnight herald a fresh start
A chance to mend wounds, heal a broken heart

In the bewitching hour, hearts intertwine
In clandestine meetings, by moonlight divine
Lovers seek solace, beneath a starlit canopy
Midnight beginnings, forging bonds endlessly

The night sky's tapestry, an opus untold
With every twinkling star, a tale to behold
Whispers of poets, their verses take flight
In the caress of midnight, their words ignite

Darkness looming thick like fog
Changes coming tadpole to frog

Caterpillar to butterfly
Reach the stars in the sky

Catacombs of the mind
Shine a light on the blind

Rest assured don't be scared
We the ones chose to be bared

No more same old new beginning
For those of us who are winning

Winning freedom winning trust
Finish line go for bust

Lower the drawbridge castle walls
Feed the children feed them all

Open access positive
keep your terror no place to give

Watch us change what we know
Watch us step up and change the show

Primary problem ignorance
studying scripture is the hint

Denial resting in its bed
Spiritually starving fear like dread

Lollygaggers laurel leaning
What's the purpose what's the meaning

On a rock somewhere unknown
Hear you calling put down your phone

Write your own story live in tune
Put away that book of doom

Test new theories truly brave
Save your own ass that you was gave

Create a conscious to be proud of
Embrace your own heart let it love

Off the sideline ready to play
Write my own rules it's my way

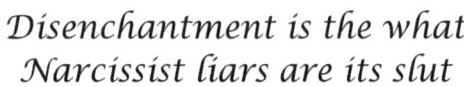

Salvation sickness lust for control
Digging humanity a deeper hole

Confiscation of the will
Paying dearly for this bill

Slavery hasn't changed
Sound the alarm cut the chains

Disenchantment is the what
Narcissist liars are its slut

Oh my gosh don't be so mean
You ain't heard nothin I'm a machine

Finally tuned precision piece
Never needing any grease

Sharp in wit laser tongue
It's our turn to become

Hey religion take a bow
Here comes the tractor and the plow

Upon the shores where angels tread
Where dreams take flight and fears are shed
A realm of beauty, pure and bright
Where heaven meets the earth's embrace, just right

The sands, a glimmering tapestry
With shells that sing the ocean's glee
Caressed by waves, a gentle dance
As sun and sea in love enhance

A symphony of colors bloom
As angels' wings the skies illume
Their radiant grace, a sight to hold
A vision of divinity untold

Soft whispers ride the ocean breeze
Their words a balm that hearts appease
They carry hopes and blessings too
To those in need, in love so true

In this sacred haven by the sea
A glimpse of heaven's mystery
Where mortal souls may find release
And earthly burdens gently cease

Beside the angel shores, we stand
In awe of this enchanted land
With every step, our spirits soar
In heaven's love forevermore

Embracing your weakness, is a strength untold
A journey within, to find your inner gold
For in our imperfections, lies a beauty rare
A path to growth, and a lesson to share

It takes courage, to accept what's true
To acknowledge, the parts of us we never knew
To see our vulnerabilities, as gifts in disguise
And harness their power, with a love in our eyes

For in embracing our weakness, we find our might
A newfound strength, that shines so bright
A confidence, that can weather any storm
And a resilience, that keeps us warm

So embrace your flaws, and all that you lack
For in doing so, a new you will crack
With a bravery, that knows no bounds
And a beauty, that astounds

For it's in embracing your weakness, you'll find
The courage to be, the true self in your mind,
So cherish your imperfections, and love what you see
For they make you, the unique and amazing person
you're meant to be

Skillful skillset plethora
Truth in meaning dilemma

Battle tested no fatigue
No one nothing out my league

Conditioned robots everywhere
Crossed up channels barely there

I'm hard wired no off switch
Don't harass me I'll make you twitch

Think I'm crazy well thank you
I remember what I can do

Positive output narrative
Dogma gone no way to live

Standard striving honestly
Own worst critic to become free

Angels dancing on my side
The time has come to provide

Red pill blue pill or free will
It's a choice or are you ill

Despite deceit and the lies
Isn't it obvious why power tries

Devious deeds in the name
Wake up fools this aint no game

Boots on the ground with its cross
One man's memory quite the cost

Proud and brave no not really
Power hungry fire in belly

Eager to conquer behind closed doors
Secrets swirling causing wars

Sold a dream live a lie
No wonder drugs keep us high

Here to hear not be told
Looking for my pot of gold

Rainbows edge leprechaun
Seeing past the scammers con

Restored memories erosion gone
Free to sing a brand new song

No more digging no more lair
It's now time to take the dare

Stepping out to right the wrongs
Colonialism and its throngs

Wiping out confiscate
All things natural perpetrate

Criminal conduct justified
History's horrors crucified

Credit where please stand up
Accept this poison in your cup

When life is good and all seems bright
And everything is going just right
It seems that others start to envy
And all their kindness starts to end, see

They see your smile, your happy heart
And it tears them apart, tears them apart
They long for what they cannot see
And envy starts to consume, gradually

They see the life you lead so well
The wealth, the love, and all that swell
And think that you have had it easy
As if life's blessings have come so breezy

But little do they know the pain
The sleepless nights, the endless strain
That you have faced to reach your goal
The sacrifices that made you whole

They envy you for the success you've gained
The love, the joy, the happiness sustained
They long for what they think is yours
But don't know the journey that brought you to the doors

So when they envy, just smile and say
It took hard work and dedication each day
And remind them that they too can find
Success and joy, with a heart and mind aligned.

Just hold on I'll be there
One more breath one more dare

It's been fated entangled souls
No time apart can fill our holes

Only together make us whole
Plug the leaks in each our soul

So many lives missing pieces
This time we can lift our species

You and me we are one
Meant to be so let's have fun

Emotional wave filled with dreams
Silenced nightmares filled with screams

Opinions silenced cauterize
The moment is now to open your eyes

Choose your path choose it wise
Turn up the volume tune out the lies

Scripture reliant no own thought
Life on the toilet is what you got

Bamboozled stagnation denigrate creed
Two thousand years of same old breed

Dirty little secrets dirty little lies
Dirty little conscience maggot laying flies

Cherry bomb nose rosacea skin
Drunk in the bar once again

Spiritually ill purpose unknown
Limp wristed weasel burying its bone

Oh you believe I don't really care
I light up the night sky with my own flare

My brightness abounds glittering gleam
This reality is not how it be seem

Ditch the pitch salvation sick
Elst I grab a bigger stick

Persecution is what I find
Throughout history has left us blind

Power players cutting off
The heads of free will rules aloft

Dirty deeds done dirt cheap
Keeping power at the top of the heap

Run for the hills if you wanna survive
When fire brother did arrive

No welcome sign stolen land
Restricted access dirty hand

No respect for the lives
Of red brother or his wives

Time to tally up the toll
Greedy heathens time to roll

Truth may be spoken, but not always heard
For lies can lurk within its every word
Like a seed that's planted deep in soil
Deceit can grow amidst the truth's toil

We think we know what's real and right
But lies can hide in plain sight
They twist and turn the facts we know
Until the truth's distorted, hidden below

We search for answers, we seek the light
But lies can shroud even the brightest sight
They mask themselves in the truth we find
And lead us down paths we've left behind

So be wary, be wise, and always beware
For lies can hide in truth's own lair
And though we strive to seek what's true
Lies can taint the very things we pursue

Speaking her mind keeping the peace
Courage to slay any a beast

Ivory tower shoes of a saint
Being herself nothing she ain't

Smiling eyes glow to her soul
What is her secret what does she know

Time for the wounded insite galore
Cleaning up messes mopping the floor

Confidence constant humble approach
Hearing the whispers without any coach

Plenty of passion to live life itself
Conscience gleaming spiritual health

Lead to the well filling her cup
Looking around saying whats up

Glad she's my friend glad that we met
My moneys on her to win the big bet

Blame blame blame back again
Never lived a day in sin

Stage is set to start the show
It's your turn your turn to grow

Cast a line to an unknown shore
See what's there to explore

Anxiety angst fear based thought
Conformity killing the melting pot

Anger brooding discontent
Not enough money to pay the rent

Dissolution the serpent smiles
Tail wagging many miles

Harbored hatred for the free
Because it knows it'll never be

Having your presence in my life
Has lifted me out of strife

Your sweet smile your loving voice
I am yours that is my choice

Holding hands we walk as one
Life is ours we have won

A once in a lifetime leap of fate
Intuition ain't it great

Crafted finally before time
The love we share creates our shine

Never lonely never scared
This leap of fate was worth the dare

Our own model made for us
All things other can eat our dust

In sunny meadows, laughter springs
Where bumblebees dance with butterfly wings
A whimsical tale, I'll now unfold
Of a merry adventure, so pure and bold

In a land of cotton candy dreams
Where rivers flow with melted ice cream
A jolly squirrel with a mischievous grin
Embarked on a quest with a twirl and a spin

With acorns as treasure, he skipped with delight
Through lollipop forests, under moonlit night
Skipping stones on marshmallow ponds
He sang silly songs, creating fond bonds

He met a wise owl, perched on a tree
Reciting riddles with utmost glee
Together they laughed, their spirits so light
Underneath stars that shimmered so bright

They climbed candy canes, oh so high
To touch the clouds drifting in the sky
Tickled by rainbows, they danced on its hue
Spreading laughter, as only they knew

They played tag with fireflies, blinking in flight
Their glow illuminating the velvety night
A game of hide-and-seek with
twinkling stars
Oh, what joyous merriment, no troubles,
no scars

Through gumdrop valleys and chocolate hills
They ventured on, giggling with thrills
Their laughter echoed, filling the air
A symphony of joy, beyond compare

Get what you give see through the lies
Ignore the noise open your eyes

Power struggle killing itself
Along with the patrons sick in health

Badges guns david's star
No respect set the bar

Covert chaos victim hood
Facts are simple wish i could

Intimidation a babies cry
Throwing stones from nearby

Chose for what false in pride
Behind its star is where they hide

Eager for money or someone's gold
Diamonds will do so I'm told

That's enough grow some balls
Something to put in your overalls

Held to the candle without a burn
Purification not a yearn

Seen it coming talking walls
The time has come for the smalls

Eager witness for the fall
Truth be told it's for us all

No more ropes no more chains
Or scrambled eggs instead of brains

All things leading down same path
Who be with me who the cast

Dopey ding dongs rule no more
We the mop you the floor

Paramedics not on site
No ones coming for your fight

End game done power has lost
Many lives was the cost

Through the fire through the rain
On the other side of pain

Didn't know didn't care
Trust in love I declare

Spiritual warrior bound to earth
Truthful and honest I give birth

Dedicated at all costs
Only one can be the boss

Whispers washing through my soul
Telling pain where to go

Reaching heights can't explain
Through self love without pain

Stoic striving strong and bold
On this love I do hold

Borrowed beliefs here and there
Work for me and now I care

Of the beauty in grace and the power she holds
Hills become flat on straight roads

Her time has come the here is now
In that soul she knows the how

Trash Talk won't distract her views
There is comfort in her shoes

Caught the break she was looking for
When wisdom came knocking on her door

Surely sincere the mirror reflects
What's in her heart she protects

One bright light in a dark night sky
The healing you seek are the tears you cry

Love blooms in shades of crimson red
Passion's fire ignites, words left unsaid
A color that evokes desire and heat
Two souls entwined, a love so sweet

In the depths of love, we find the blue
A tranquil hue, where serenity grew
Like a calm ocean, love's waves embrace
Whispering promises, in this peaceful space

Yellow, the color of sunshine and light
Love's radiance, a beacon shining bright
It illuminates hearts with joy and cheer
Dispelling darkness, bringing love near

Purple, the color of mystery and dreams
Love's enchantment, woven in secret schemes
A mystical hue, where hearts entwine
In a dance of love, so sublime

Orange, vibrant and full of zest
Love's energy, a passion manifest
It sparks excitement, ignites the flame
In this fiery love, we're never the same

Pink, a color of tenderness and affection
Love's gentle touch, a sweet connection
Soft petals of love, delicately unfurled
Creating a love story, the envy of the world

So let love's colors blend and intertwine
Creating a masterpiece, divine
For love, in all its shades and hues
Paints a canvas, where hearts find their cues

Melancholy kind of place
At the end of the race

Cruise control parts replaced
Steady hands steady pace

Valley highway nice and straight
Path is clear hard to wait

Last location rearview mirror
Next destination to where i steer

Another challenge another test
With one key I'll do my best

So much silence after the pain
Nothing nowhere was in vein

Erosion eating at the soul
It's your turn your turn to grow

Strength within responsible
Smash the pedal start to roll

Old a feeble not feeling well
Told me eyez goin to hell

Walk in my shoes just for a while
And you will see why I must smile

I didn't do it, it wasn't me
I was hiding in a tree

Pointing fingers whose around
Can't blame those in the ground

Stretch the truth just a bit
Sure to make that narrative fit

Beckoning brandish holy ghost
That thing makes me laugh the most

Murder for freedom while they attack
Waiting for cowards to stab in the back

Surely not right honor defense
Counting the scalps on the fort fence

Promise ring anchoring chain
Society's way to intensify pain

Promising falsehood conformities way
Keep us in line making us pay

Rebellious and young our future not theirs
Who is with me who does dares

Break from the cycle break form the bond
Follow your heart feel it respond

Terrified to lose control
It's your life its your soul

Possession taken criminals
This a culture full of holes

They do like you where you are
But there's so much I see so far

See the future be the one
Really I'm a lot of fun

In a world of chaos and strife, I confess
A blessing emerges, standing strong, no less
Like armor forged, unyielding and bold
A bulletproof blessing, a story untold

In moments of doubt, it shields the soul
A sanctuary of grace that makes us whole
No matter the tempest, no matter the fight
The blessing prevails, shining in its might

It fortifies hearts, a shield against pain
Infusing strength, flowing through every vein
When darkness descends, and shadows prevail
The bulletproof blessing is a holy grail

With unwavering faith, it guides our way
A compass of hope, come what may
Through battles fought and trials faced
The blessing remains, unwavering, encased

It weaves through our lives, like a sacred thread
Mending brokenness, healing wounds that bled
A divine gift bestowed upon our hearts
An armor of love that never departs

In times of despair, it offers release
A tender embrace, granting inner peace
Through every hardship, it stands unbroken
A testament to the power of words
unspoken

In my thoughts you are here
By my side as a steer

Not a wobble no side track
Free to live life not in wack

Soldering forward ambition grand
Courageous for the last stand

Strength in love separation none
Join my world for endless fun

Medicine through love laughter too
We the future we the who

No one coming to save your ass
Ditch religion let their pain pass

Butchery of what's so great
Dogma demon corrupted fate

Look I love us we are kind
Find the courage don't be blind

Bashful and shy looking so hot
Nothing left out all that she got

Amazing presence mesmerized
Sparkle in each of eyes

Innocent laughter out of her shell
Playful and fun beautiful smell

Long flowing hair soft as it gets
We don't talk about those tits

Real earth angel here to shine
In the flesh I've gone blind

Every feature every curve
All uncanny here to serve

Beacon light house on the shore
She's got beauty I can't ignore

Who be next
To remove the boot from our necks

Tear down the walls
that hold on to our balls

High as fuck but not on drugs
Kicking ass on the thugs

Bring it bitch I got tools
Not the ones held by fools

Confidence no coincidence
Gloves be off for the stance

Trust me try me kiss my ass
Drink your poison from your own glass

At home where I'm beacon of hope
Untying knots in a long rope

Broken eggs everywhere
Dumb and blind sit and stare

In glass houses without a shield
Reaping nothing without yield

Slaves of corporate America
Institutions of the duh

Denial in the dogma can't accept my truth
Peel back your eyes and listen to the proof

Within each egg at its core
Is what humanity is looking for

Ostentatious yes I know
But I have come to tell you so

So hurry up don't be lame
Get off your couch stop laying blame

It's our time we are great
Cut the head off the snake

Inadequate knowledge wisdom slim
Every Sunday same old hymn

Testicle tied to a cross
Nuteur the people show them who's boss

Rotten eggs spoiled head
Garden full of the dead

Testimony triggered without scare
Yes I said it how do I dare

No I'm not judging just here to say
Religion is poison causing decay

On the wrong path perpetuating lies
I know my truth look deep in my eyes

The deepest of oceans bottomless pond
I am inspired I got a deep bond

Yours to have but not without tears
Get off your ass and face your own fears

Why hide the beauty inside

Let it out lay waste to doubt

Deal in dreams not in screams

Hold on to trust buff off the rust

False ego fails whales with no tails

Scavengers careen with motives unseen

Egotistic trials false in its smiles

Mask of some beast served up at the feast

Packaged in pain all strides in vein

Holy regret lifeless secret

Paralyzing lies open your eyes

Confident I cry I say goodbye

Painting in the park long after dark

Canvas in my head exposing what's been red

Visions filled with joy like a brand new toy

Revival in the soul sturdy here I go

Seeing through BS in this vision I caress

Situation seems it's time to be redeemed

Trade old for the new who the fuck are you

Corrected through self love
Wisdom from above

Behaving how I speak
Enjoyment at its peak

Vision in the glory
Timeless in its story

Suspended in freight agendas delight

Criminal cause without laws

No low too low history's the know

Reform no good wish that I could

Express what we are
Words they seem far

Insane asylum for the weak
Spirituality for the meek

Keys of peter in my hand
Ready to renew the land

Feel the vibe am I clear
It won't be long the new is near

Mother nature speaking out
I hear her cries without a doubt

We her patient she our nurse
She tires of the open purse

Safe to say no one knows
I only know my own flows

I see inside the smoke and mirrors
Even when I'm drinking beers

Many will gawk some will see
But only the pure will be set free

Maybe me maybe not
But can't forget what I got

Killing anger by being kind
Just don't cross me and alls be fine

Territory of thee unknown
Is where I find myself at home

Torch to light the funeral fire
Of the church and their desire

Old guard gone don't know where
All who left stand and stare

Shivers running down the spine
I've been waiting for this time

Imagination turned to gold
Never before big and bold

Ending war and the pain
Religious conflict is the blame

Don't admit it no longer care
Life is nothing but a dare

Dare to reach the pinnacle
of the heart space and the soul

No longer hiding from my truth
Eating breakfast in the next booth

All for one and one for all
Echoes through a joyous hall

Vibrations of goodness surrounded by hope
Change the ingredient to play a new note

Drum of creation subtle and sweet
Calling us back when we complete

Fantastic in design brilliant in plan
Winds of change are coming I am a real fan

Reality altered hard to explain
Punch your own ticket to ride this train

Excuses expired no tardy ness
All aboard on the one way party express

Humility and humor requirement
No more anger no reason to vent

Do your own work think for yourself
What is your purpose how is your health

Only saying it's my job
I'll be safe from the mob

Play it safe stay in line
Letting religion steal your shine

Confiscation of your true gift
Falling victim to the grift

Mutilation spirit and soul
Ugly hiding like a troll

Gobbling goblin in the mind
Scripture stripping back divine

Codependent give it up
Let your own self fill your own cup

No more half empty no more half full
Spilling over from the well

Echoed memories of a time
Before religion and its shrine

Favor lost out of greed
Scorching the earth poisoned seed

Nervous losers have no chance
Your evil magic can't touch this dance

Old world baggage rotten smell
No wonder Christians created hell

Power struggle nothing new
Killed their own martyr jew

I know how dare I
I was there to watch him die

Resurrection mushroom trip
Top of the triangle from its tip

Power trippin on its lies
Man on cross its disguise

Trinity theory and its cause
Justification and conformity laws

Not our purpose to be tied up
Chained to its laws and a broken cup

A slide of hand deceptions crown
Giving its crowd a sad like frown

Eagerly waiting for one mans return
While laying claim others will burn

Marketed and packaged all nice and neat
Brought to your doorstep dropped at your feet

A broken package contents spoiled
Here to lay claim much has been foiled

Contrived and altered by power and greed
Conformities purpose to steal all good seed

I stand and deliver this truth of mine
This is my message I know I'm not blind

Redefining who we are
Out on the plains to heal the scar

Heartbeat pounds to the sounds

Universe keeps calling when I'm falling

Torn and tattered life don't matter

Wanna go home to the home I've known

Looking for courage to get through this purge

Tested again to find deep within

Fighting off pain that I must remain

Gotta keep going all's I be knowing

Please take my hand to make this last stand

Heart medicine vitamin L
Apparently it might keep us from hell

Creatures of habit good or bad
Whatever seems to be the new fad

Lost in the vision the purpose to be
Happy healthy loving and free

Guilty of one thing having fun
Free to roam out under the sun

Experience explains powers place
Tearing apart the whole human race

High on itself no low to low
Causing humanity to live in its woe

Greedy and corrupt never enough
The hill we all climb shouldn't be so tough

Will fighting will power on top
Influencing society who's ready to pop

*Exposing the light to evils wrongs
How religion holds with thongs*

*Mistake or on purpose don't really care
But won't admit it no matter the scare*

*Keeps holding on this present day
Clouds of dishonor guilty I'd say*

*Freedom of thought cut off the head
Lay waste to the neighbor all who have bled*

*Authority of terror not of the light
Forgiveness is over to my delight*

*Know me feel me hear my words
Religion made us into turds*

*But there's hope sovranty
If you really wanna be free*

*Lol what a joke
Religion have another toke*

Heart wide open taking it in
Trying not to let it get trampled again

A life worth living exposing lies
Each one with its own surprise

Painful yes but what a ride
These days i just seem to glide

Like a free fall to the stars
Tethered to source healed from scars

In my element chameleon
Wishing change could replace sin

Aerogent authority go away
Your days are over you got no play

Not here to suffer in your world
Here to light up and stir the soul

Go back to the stone age where you belong
Hit that hashish in your hookah bong

Bamboozled by power not the light
Freedom is ours and worth the fight

In word we turn to what's in our hearts
Take care of your body all of its parts

Love yourself and be kind
Kill the anger with your shine

Bury the hatchet with your love
Vibrate with the wings above

Sovereignty our truest gift
Be the next to expose the grift

Locked and lonely hearts desire
To the top I aspire

On the rebound dignity intact
Not pointing fingers because that is wack

Taking all in choices to choose
Finally walking in my own shoes

Breathless in betrayal pounding in my head
Hung out on a limb memories I dread

Toxic in temptations acting innocent
Just like the beginning of histories decent

Baby in the bath water boiled to well done
No religious dogma is any fun

So I carve my own path
No fear to pour from my own Krath

Diligent I move to this angelic groove

Stop you're killing me Damn I gotta pee

Clean up crew neck deep in goo

Cancerous sores dead dying horse

Forgetful and arthritic never did get it

Shameful at birth devouring the earth

Cuddling its kind righteous and blind

Cocked to go off false ego with cough

Chakras closed anger and fear imposed

Negative nellies with big bellies

Covered in soot darkness has put

Ridiculous story speaking of glory

Martyrs abound is what was found

Persecute the pure death the cure

Exploitation of earth and child
In a zoo not the wild

Where to credit what's gone wrong
Why must we sing another sad song

Gripping reality counting the dots
Of the haves and the nots

Justly judging corrupted crown
On a spiral heading down

Herded cattle naked sheep
Falling in line without a peep

Clothes line dried after the ring
Living a life that didn't mean a thing

Wreckless abuse verbalized
Seeking power to paralyze

Source not important with same goals
Creating victims with big holes

Closing out closing down
Our open hearts and creative crown

Hyper sensitive squealing belts
Blocking channels with ugly welts

Critical thinking been shut off
Forcing feeding from a trough

Balance burned emotions scorched
By controls flaming torch

In a world that never shuts off
Each a moment to cure our cough

Words and thoughts emanate
As we determine our own fate

Tied to get there by mysteries mist
From the very first true kiss

Set intentions carry through
Keep resolutions if just a few

Carry kindness let it flow
Let this feeling live and grow

Be the spark honor the path
Live in the moment don't let it pass

Never again will I share
That loving touch and caring stare

Broken and bound to tragedies grip
Twenty years sober might need a slip

The greatest gift to live in love
Encased in a glow from above

Satisfaction stripped away
As I cry here everyday

Not enough words to explain the loss
Everything always has its cost

Born to shine groomed to fail
On my head falls softball hail

One more test no humor involved
Whatever it takes to evolve

Bludgeoned by books writings contain
What we have now and its stain

Never what was meant to be
Not a slave state of conformity

Daily diet of some false hope
Evil empire of the pope

Looking back seeing through
The true purpose of religious spue

Cornered now no place to run
Will fight to the death with spear and gun

Legions will follow to death's door
Forgetting the love that's at our core

A fateful trip yes indeed
But in love there will be no need

Deceiving unpleasant decadence
Always preceding upsetting events

Extraordinary unresolved human flaws
Manipulated for wrong cause

Mic drop moment step on up
Who wants credit for each broken cup

Leaders of division the coward's cloak
Around the neck they do choke

Quite the descendants at all costs
Force conformity on the conquered and lost

In the name of whichever one
As each empire has always done

Rare event around the bend
That will be controls end

Here comes the hatchet to sever ties
Of what is truth and what is lies

Based on the reality that warlords made
Each and every soul have paid

Black mail extortion debauchery
Claiming authority over the free

Sickening insight to what's been hid
Since I was a little kid

Love me hate me nothing new
Jealous hater smell like poo

Lightning striking to destroy
An evil empire and its ploy

The mask is off and what's revealed
Is a rotten onion long since peeled

Rebellious message above critique
Making strong out of the weak

Attila Ghangas and Brave heart
Fighting oppression of conformity's dart

Strung up strung out cauterized
Enforcing the rules of blind eyes

Captivating concepts theories flawed
Oppress the oppressor chilling cause

Rebounding history planning plans
Consolidating power into few hands

Media meltdowns spreading distrust
Feeding narratives of disgust

Clergy sidesteps honest speech
To this level they'll never reach

Harbinger of truth and love that's real
Preparing humanity to get off the triangular wheel

Inner shadows enforced by crooks
Codependent on their books

Playing out a plan of nefarious power
Creating victims every hour

Held in esteem freewill removed
Pointing a finger back to ones grove

Stripped of oneness in human acts
Head on a block here comes the ax

Proclaiming ownership of what's to come
Through salvation is quite dumb

What was promised has been gave
With our blood we have paid

Time to stop the fractured lies
Time to clear our blood shot eyes

Stolen cultures destructive ways
Weak and innocence always pays

Crafty con-men cultivate
Ill intentions to stagnate

Progressive party go get laid
In your ugly twisted ways

Consolidation same old shit
Forcing families to suck the tit

Could have made you happy could have had it all
The first the last never let you fall

Soaked in satin pure like snow
How could I ever let you go

Angel eyes glowing skin
Button pushed to begin

Halo mindset with the skills
Of the heart space as it spills

Turning heads watching close
She the one with the most

Internal clock set to chime
The second after I finish this rhyme

Accountable knowing responsible
Doing whatever to free the soul

Heaving heavy to lighten the load
Shifting onto a less traveled road

Events unfolding magnetic flow
Hooked on the wisdom that I known

Braced to carry and travel on
No time like the present to be upon

Lying mouths unseen eyes
Hiding cowards no surprise

Alert dexterity driving home
Cosmic awakening attuning tone

Pressed to service ring the bell
Lit to light and to tell

Navigating a treacherous sea
One of storms emotionally

Tricked to abandon the heart space glow
Wrecked in anger that I used to know

Tidal wave of anxiety
Blinded by what I see

Bilge pumps purging sinking ship
Damn this life is such a trip

Desert isle moonlit beach
Trust through wisdom is where I reach

Anchor cut loose set a float
This place is perfect to promote

Back to basics drawing board
Left to vices not the hoard

Lifted gifted and gettin down
Standing clear of the merry go round

Can't return to the life that was
Of the toxic fuzzy fuzz

Free will flowing el natural
Favorable wind to fill my sail

Can't explain what won't make sense
So I stay thankful for this chance to dance

Awareness adding lost and found
Shaving weight pound by pound

One big smile for my birth
As to leave love on this earth

Free me from this pain I feel
Make me strong so I can heal

Imprint your name into my soul
Fix the wounds fill in the whole

Laugh with me while I sleep
Be my first thought as a reap

Sense my being lift my hope
Wash my back with ivory soap

Cling to my side watch over me
Teach me life and how to see

Grant the gifts bestowed on earth
Let my gestures give new hope birth

Hold the enemy in your palm
Don't let anyone drop the bomb

Cold blooded version of what I can't take
Eyes of beauty tongue of a snake

Energy wasted moving on
15 years flushed down the jon

Broken heart no more tears
Not holding space for mine and hers

Not my loss did my best
Not gonna keep this on my chest

Starting over again and again
Maybe next I'll get that win

Knock me down I get back up
Won't let this setback keep me stuck

Foundation blown up won't rebuild
Will find a new field with dirt untilled

Held up to see or see through
Dismantling the illusion that keeps us blue

Floppy stories authority obsessed
Laying what's not theirs on the already blessed

Prayer for power in climatic cause
Traumatic reckoning to universe and laws

Nowhere to run nowhere to hide
On a slope with a slippery slide

Backwaters brackish stagnant and dark
Try and get out for a walk I the park

Clarity blurred festering lies
Hard to explain what will be a surprise

Patchwork of persons strategically placed
Bringing back what power erased

Dedicated to: The Unblind

Seekers of answers time has come
To heal the collective from its numb

Oppositions power will shatter in truth
This is for real not just some goof

Our hearts are together filled with source
We riding in on a white horse

These energies lift us to new heights
Keeping us strong for any a fights

Our purpose has come our love leads the way
Rising the conscience for a bright new day

With hurt melted off who we once were
No one's burden could ever be a cure

www.ingramcontent.com/pod-product-compliance
Lightning Source LLC
LaVergne TN
LVHW041708060526
838201LV00043B/632